PEGASUS ENCYCLOPEDIA LIBRARY

Continents
SOUTH AMERICA

Edited by: Pallabi B. Tomar, Hitesh Iplani
Managing editor: Tapasi De
Designed by: Vijesh Chahal, Anil Kumar, Rohit Kumar
Illustrated by: Suman S. Roy, Tanoy Choudhury
Colouring done by: Vinay Kumar, Kiran Kumari & Pradeep Kumar

CONTENTS

Introduction

South America is the southern continent of the Americas. It is located to the south of the equator that is why it is called South America. It is the world's fourth largest continent.

The continent has a total of 12 independent countries—Argentina, Bolivia, Brazil, Chile, Colombia, Ecuador, Guyana, Paraguay, Peru, Suriname, Uruguay, Venezuela. The French Guiana falls under the control of the French government.

South America stretches approximately 7,640 km from Punta Gallinas (Colombia) in the north to Cape Horn (Chile) in the south. It is approximately 5,300 km wide from east to west at its broadest point.

South America is connected to North America by the **Isthmus of Panama**.

Countries of South America

	Flag	Name	Capital	Official language(s)	Currency
1.		Argentina	Buenos Aires	Spanish	Argentine pesos
2.		Bolivia	La Paz & Sucre	Spanish, Quechua, Aymara	Boliviano
3.		Brazil	Brasília	Portuguese	Real
4.		Chile	Santiago	Spanish	Chilean pesos
5.		Colombia	Bogotá	Spanish	Colombian pesos
6.		Ecuador	Quito	Spanish	US dollar
7.		Guyana (under French govt.)	Georgetown	English	Guyanese dollars
8.		Paraguay	Asunción	Spanish, Guaraní	Guarani

9.		Peru	Lima	Spanish, Quechua	Nuevo sol
10.		Suriname	Paramaribo	Dutch	Surinamese dollars
11.		Trinidad and Tobago	Port of Spain	English	Trinidad and Tobago dollars
12.		Uruguay	Montevideo	Spanish	Uruguayan pesos
13.		Venezuela	Caracas	Spanish	Bolivars

Geography

Location

The Caribbean Sea is located above the continent in the northwest. The Atlantic Ocean surrounds it in the east, and the Pacific Ocean surrounds it in the west. It is separated from Antarctica by the Drake Passage.

The continent covers an area of 17,821,028 sq km accounting for approximately 12 per cent of the surface area of the earth.

The landscape of South America can be divided into three main regions. The Andes Mountains line the west coast forming a backbone down the entire length of the continent; the highlands and plateaus in the east are the oldest geological feature of the continent; and dense rainforests in the humid Amazon valley and along the Caribbean coast cover much of the north and northeast.

South America at a glance

Number of countries	12
Largest country	Brazil, 8,511,965 sq km
Smallest country	Suriname, 161,470 sq km
Largest lake	Lake Titicaca, Bolivia/Peru, 8,340 sq km
Longest river	Amazon, 6, 439 km
Highest point	Cerro Aconcagua, Argentina, 6,959 m
Major deserts	Atacama Desert, Chile

The Andes

The Andes

The great mountain range of South America is the Andes Mountains, which extends more than 7, 250 km all the way down the western coast of the continent. The highest peak of the Andes called Mount Aconcagua is on the western side of central Argentina, and is 6,959 m high.

Eastern Highlands

The Eastern Highlands and plateaus are the oldest geological region of South America. The Eastern Highlands can be divided into three main sections—**the Guiana Highlands, the Brazilian Highlands and the Patagonian Highlands**.

The Guiana Highlands cover the Guianan states, southern Venezuela and north-eastern Brazil. It is in this region in Venezuela that the highest waterfall of the world, **Angel Falls,** is located.

Amazon Basin

The Amazon River forms the Amazon Basin which is the largest basin in the world, covering an area of about 7 million sq km. The Amazon jungle covers most of the Amazon Basin.

The basin was once an enormous bay, before the Andes were pushed up along the coasts the Amazon. As the mountain range grew, they held back the ocean and eventually the bay became an inland sea.

River Amazon

This sea was finally filled by the erosion of the higher land surrounding it and finally a huge plain, crisscrossed by countless waterways, was created. Most of this region is still at the sea level and is covered by lush jungle and extensive wetlands.

Mineral deposits

A lot of mineral deposits, particularly copper, silver and gold are found in the Andes. In Venezuela, the Andes are mined for lead, petroleum, phosphates, copper and salt.

Columbia is rich in deposits of coal and is the largest producer of gold and platinum in South America. Columbia is also rich in emeralds, with the second largest deposits of emeralds in the world.

In Chile, the Andes are mined primarily for copper in addition to lead, zinc, and silver.

Amazonian forest

Bolivia has huge tin mines. The Andes here are a source of tungsten, antimony, nickel, chromium, cobalt and sulphur.

The Amazon jungle is the largest rainforest of the world and is on the top of the list of the New 7 Wonders of Nature which is to be declared in the year 2011.

Climate

The climate of South America is mostly wet and hot. However, due to the large size of the continent the climate varies with each region having its own characteristic weather conditions.

The Amazon River basin has the typical hot wet climate suitable for the growth of rain forests. The Andes Mountains, on the other hand, remain cold throughout the year. The Andean regions of Ecuador, Peru and Bolivia experience the driest and coldest time of the year from May to November.

The desert regions of Chile, also known as Atacama Desert, is the driest part of South America. The moisture-laden winds coming from the west shed their moisture on the western parts of the Andes, thus the eastern portions of the mountains receive very little rainfall. The cold Peru Current is responsible for the dry coastal parts of Peru as well as northern Chile.

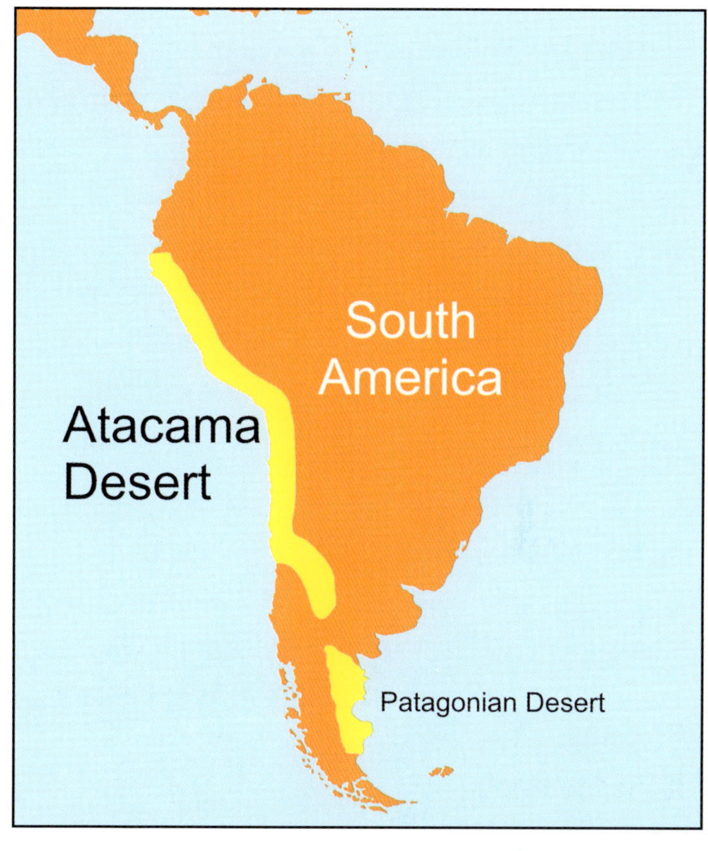

The four parts of South America which experience heavy rainfall are the Amazon River Basin, coastal parts of French Guiana, Guyana and Suriname, the south-western parts of Chile and Columbia and Ecuador coasts.

Atacama Desert

Astonishing fact

The Atacama Desert is one of the driest places of the world.

Two weather phenomena affecting the climate of South America along with the world's climate are **El Niño** and **La Niña**.

When the winds are slow the temperatures of the eastern Pacific surface rise leading to a phenomena called **El Niño**. The event results in an abnormal warming of the surface of ocean waters in the eastern Pacific. Also, it is the cause of extreme weather conditions such as floods, droughts and other weather disturbances in many parts of the world.

While on the other hand when strong winds appear, the circulation of air currents over the ocean increases and the temperatures in the eastern Pacific Ocean decreases. This phenomenon is known as **La Niña**.

Temperature

The climate of South America varies widely over a large range of altitudes and latitudes, and only in isolated regions is the temperature range greater than about 20°C.

The coldest part of the continent is in the extreme southern tip in the area called Tierra del Fuego; in the coldest month of the year, which is July, it is as cold as 0°C. The highest temperatures of South America have been recorded in Gran Chaco in Argentina, with temperatures going up to 43° Celsius. However, the average temperature in the same area for the hottest month of the year, which is January, is about 29°C.

Quibdo in Columbia receives the maximum rainfall. It receives an annual rainfall of 890 cm.

Devastation caused by EL Niña

History

The first inhabitants of South America who crossed the Bering Strait in prehistoric time some12, 000 to 14,000 years ago were probably of Asian descent.

The coming of Europeans

Christopher Columbus reached South America in 1498 during his third voyage from Spain to the New World. He was the first European to reach South America. Spanish conquistadors soon reached South America after Columbus established colonies and to search for silver and gold.

The civilization of the Inca Empire in South America was the most magnificent civilization of that time. It arose in about 3rd century A.D.

Slowly, most parts of the continent were conquered and were established as Spanish South America. Spanish South America was ruled as the king's private property. From the 16th to the early 19th century, it was governed by a complex administrative system.

Christopher Columbus

Roman Catholic missionaries were a powerful force in the colonial era. They established many missions among the Indians. The English, French and Dutch established settlements in the northeast.

Independence from colonial rule

Towards the end of the 18th century the unrest among the natives of the land was rising which led to frequent uprisings. Most of these uprisings were led by **creoles** (people of mixed European and black descent), who did not like Spain's tight control over their economy and politics and revolted.

The year 1810 saw the rise of various revolutionary movements in most of Spanish South America. Total independence was achieved in 1825, after a series of ferocious wars

Latin America

South America is not the same as Latin America. Latin America includes the continent of South America as well as Mexico, Central America and the Caribbean, countries which are geographically part of North America, except for Belize. All of these groups speak languages that evolved from Latin, thus the term Latin America. South America however refers to the continent. The term 'Latin America' is more an indicator of a common culture shared by the people of these countries than a geographical demarcation.

Latin America

Religion

The people who lived in the South America before the arrival of the Spanish explorers in the 16th century C.E. were **polytheistic**, that is, they worshipped many different gods including gods represented by animal idols such as jaguars and snakes. All of the Latin American and South American religious traditions involved animal sacrifice and in some cases human sacrifice as well.

Ancient South American religion consisted primarily of the Incan religious tradition. Most of the Incan rituals and beliefs were centered upon agriculture, ritual and devotion to the gods. A central practice of this religion was the worship of the sun. In the Incan religion, the god of creation was also important.

Temples and shrines played a significant role in the ancient Incan religion, often housing not only the objects of ritual and worship but also the priests, their assistants and the chosen women. Even though the religious relics were stored inside the temples, the actual religious rituals and ceremonies often took places outside.

Machu Picchu

Two important practices within ancient Incan religion were **divination** and **sacrifice**. Divination was used to predict the outcome of battles, diagnose and heal sickness, and determine which sacrifice should be made to which god at what time. Sacrifice was essential to Incan worship and included llamas, guinea pigs, certain foods, cocoa and even humans.

In the 16th century the Portuguese and the Spanish conquered Latin America and banned the native religions and imposed Catholicism on them. In case of some civilizations, despite their destruction, many cults, continued to survive in some form.

Guinea pig

Llamas

Roman Catholicism was brought to South America by the conquerors during the first part of the 16 century. During the colonial period most of the native peoples of the continent with the exception of those in the Amazon Basin, on the Pampas and in Patagonia, were converted to this faith. The overwhelming majority of the people on the continent today are Roman Catholics.

Today Latin America is a place where very different religions coexist. Christians, Muslims, Hindus, Buddhists, adherents of East Asian traditions, as well as new religions and the remains of ancient traditions, are all a part of the religiously diverse life of the continent.

Rio Carnival

Festivals

Carnival, Rio de Janeiro, Brazil

In February, a week before the start of Lent, Mardi gras is celebrated in many towns in Argentina and Brazil. The Carnival in Brazil, which is a part of the celebration of Mardi Gras, is a wild four-day celebration, which has a religious and cultural significance. Essentially it's a time of jubilation where people dance, sing and have lots of fun. Some parties last all day and night and they take over the entire city culminating in the Rio Carnival Parade. Most of the action is out on the streets with the **blocos** (flatbed trucks with bands and music systems) leading people on a 3-day dance through the streets.

Fiesta de San Juan Bautista, Venezuela

St John the Baptist is the patron saint of many people on the central Caribbean coast and they celebrate the Saint's feast day from June 23 to June 25 along with the beating of African drums.

Boi Bumba, Brazil

The Boi Bumba comes to life in late June for three nights as a scintillating spectacle of sight and sound that needs to be seen to be believed. Boi Bumba is best celebrated at the Amazonian island of Parintins in Brazil.

Boi Bumba, Brazil

Carnaval Blancos Negros, Colombia

This Columbian Carnival takes place in town of Pasto - Nariño, Colombia on January 5 and 6 every year. January 5 is the day of the black people and January 6 is the day of the white people. The parades start on January 4 with the celebration of the 'Arrival of the Castañeda Family' from Spain. People paint their faces white or black to subvert the former 'coloniser-colonised' relationship between the black and the white people. This South American festival was originally a holiday for the slaves on plantations.

Inti Raymi

Inti Raymi (The Sun Festival), Peru

This traditional Inca festival takes place on June 24 in Cuzco, Peru. An actor plays the Inca Emperor called Sapa and parades on a golden chariot through streets filled with music, prayers and dancers to the top of a hill surrounded the worshipped and revered animals of the time—condors and snakes. Later a false sacrifice of a llama heart is made and then bonfires and fireworks spark off the party that winds back through the streets.

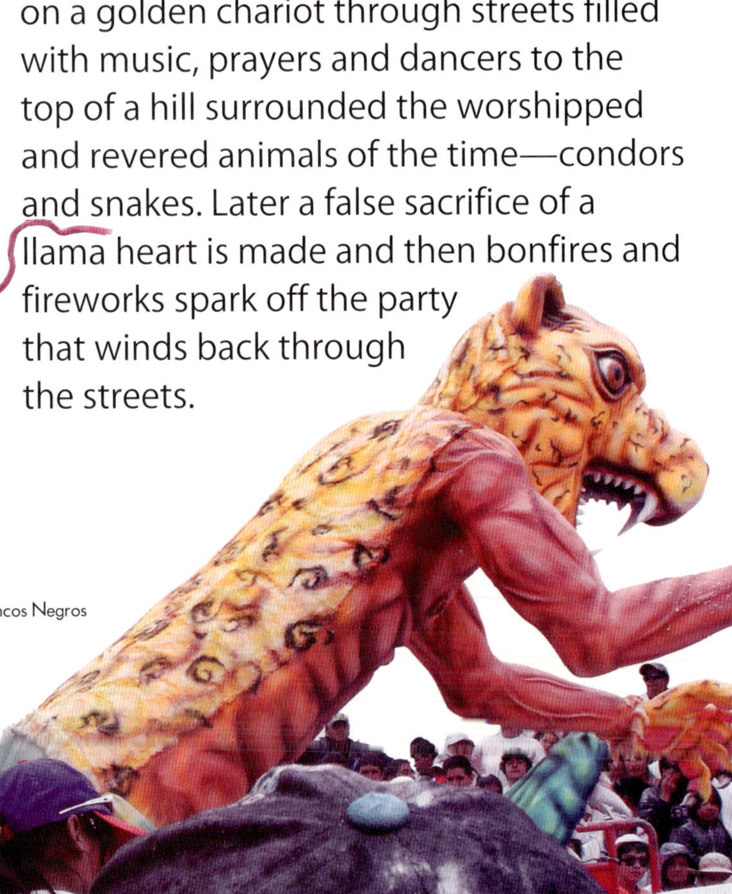

Carnaval Blancos Negros

The beautiful Salar de Uyuni is the world's largest flat salt water lake. It measures 10.582 square km and is located in the southwest of Bolivia at 3.650 m above the sea level.

The Fiesta Grande Andacollo

This is a South American fiesta which usually takes place from December 24-26 in the town of Andacollo in Central Chile. The Fiesta Grande Andacollo ceremonies include religious dances by traditional dancers, cockfighting, horseracing, food markets and drinking.

The festival celebrates the miracles of the Virgen Del Rosario and the Niño Dios de Sotaquí : Christ Child of Sotaqui.

The Guatemalan Burning Devil Festival, Guatemala

It is a religious festival which takes place on December 7, across Guatemala. In the evening around 6 pm heaps of waste and giant images of the Devil are burnt to do away with evil of any sort. People also clean their houses, cars and other belongings.

The Guatemalan Burning Devil Festival

Mes Morado

Mes Morado, Peru

Mes Morado is a festival full of processions and feasts which is celebrated throughout the month of October all over Peru particularly in Lima. Almost all the people of the country come out on the streets wearing purple coloured clothes to celebrate.

The festival of Washing-the-Bonfim-Church, Brazil

The festival is celebrated on the second Thursday after January 6, at the Church of the Bonfim, in the lower town of Salvador de Bahia, Brazil. People come and clean the church and afterwards there is an 8 km procession through the streets followed by a parade filled with lots of music and dancing. The festival lasts for ten days.

Washing-the-Bonfim

Famous people of South America

The history of Latin America is filled with lots of influential people—dictators, rulers, rebels, reformers, artists and entertainers. A few of the people who played an important role in the formation of the history of South America are:

Simón Bolívar

Simón Bolívar

Simón Bolívar (1783-1830), popularly known as the '**George Washington of South America**', led the way to freedom for millions of South Americans. He was one of South America's greatest generals. He is also known as the **El Liberator** (The Liberator). He is responsible for the independence of nations like Bolivia, Panama, Colombia, Ecuador, Peru, and Venezuela. Upper Peru became a separate state, named Bolivia in his honour in 1825. He drew up a constitution for Bolivia which is another one of his most important political contributions.

Augusto Pinochet

Augusto Pinochet (1915-2006), took control of the nation (Chile) in 1973 after leading a rebellion that ended the regime of the elected leader Salvador Allende. He was one of the leading figures in Operation Condor, an effort to intimidate and murder opposition leaders.

For almost 20 years, he ruled Chile with a strict and cruel discipline. He was responsible for the murders and executions of thousands of opposition leaders and members. On one hand he saved Chile from communism and put it on the path to modernity and on another he was a cruel, evil monster who was responsible for the deaths of many innocent men and women.

Augusto Pinochet

Fidel Castro

Fidel Castro (1926 - till date**)**, the fiery revolutionary who turned into a hot-tempered statesman has had a profound effect on world politics for fifty years. He was one of the primary leaders of the Cuban revolution. He also served as the prime minister of Cuba from 1959 to 1976. He has been an inspirational figure for people against imperialism.

Gabriel García Márquez

Gabriel García Márquez (1927 - till date), is a Nobel Prize winning writer whose novel **Hundred Years of Solitude** encompassed the amazing and magical history of Latin America. His works have been translated into dozens of languages and have sold millions of copies.

Edison Arantes do Nascimento 'Pelé'

Edison Arantes do Nascimento 'Pelé' (1940 - till date), is widely regarded as the greatest soccer player of all time. He is also known as the 'black diamond'. He has been named the 'football player of the century.' Pelé later became famous for his work for the upliftment of Brazil's poor and downtrodden and as an ambassador for soccer.

Rigoberta Menchú

A native of the rural province of Quiché, Guatemala, **Rigoberta Menchú** (1959 - till date) and her family were involved in the bitter struggle for indigenous rights. She rose to prominence in 1982 when her biography was written by Elizabeth Burgos.

Menchú turned the resulting international attention into a platform for activism and she was awarded the 1992 Nobel Peace Prize. She continues to be a world leader in native rights.

Diego Maradona

Diego Maradona

Diego Maradona (1960 - till date) too, like Pele, is considered to be a great football player. Born in Argentina, he entered the world of professional football at the young age of 15. He was selected for the national team when he was 16. He has appeared in 4 FIFA World Cup Tournaments.

Cesar Pelli

Cesar Pelli (1926 - till date) has been declared as one of the most influential living American architects by the American Institute of Architects (AIA). He has designed some of the most remarkable buildings ranging from high-rise office towers to private homes. Some of his famous works are the San Bernardino City Hall in San Bernardino, California; the Pacific Design Centre in Los Angeles, California; the United States Embassy in Tokyo, Japan; and the World Financial Centre and Winter Garden at Battery Park, New York, which has been hailed as one of the ten best works of American architecture designed since 1980.

Cesar Pelli

Pablo Neruda (Neftalí Ricardo Reyes Basoalto)

Pablo Neruda (1904-1973) is one of the greatest poets of Latin America. He was also a politician. He won the Nobel Prize for literature in 1971.

Ernesto 'Che' Guevara

Ernesto Guevara de la Serna (1928), popularly known as Che Guevara, was an important leader in the Cuban Revolution and later an important figure in the Cuban government. After completing his medical studies at the University of Buenos Aires, Guevara became a political activist first in Argentina, his native country, and then in neighbouring Bolivia and Guatemala.

He fought against imperialism in all of its forms for which he is highly honoured. However, he is also greatly hated because of his militant ways. He was captured and executed in Bolivia by CIA trained Bolivian Green Berets in the late 60's, after a failed revolution attempt.

Since his death, Guevara has become a legendary figure. His name is often equated with rebellion revolution and socialism.

Famous cities of South America

Buenos Aires

Buenos Aires, Argentina

Big, sprawling **Buenos Aires**, the capital of Argentina, is cosmopolitan and yet retains a neighbourhood feel. Buenos Aires is one of the largest cities in the world. It is also one of the most elegant and busy cities in South America. The city has managed to preserve old traditions and charm. This port city has been the gateway to Argentina for centuries.

Rio de Janeiro, Brazil

Rio de Janeiro was discovered on January 1, 1502 by Portuguese sailors who mistook the entrance of Guanabara Bay for the mouth of a river (Rio). In the 18 century it became a major shipping port for gold and diamonds.

Rio de Janeiro has a majestic beauty with areas nestled between a magnificent bay and dazzling beaches on one side and an abruptly rising mountain range covered by a luxuriant tropical forest on the other. This unique landscape makes Rio one of the most beautiful cities in the world, justifying its title of 'Marvelous City' (Cidade Maravilhosa).

It has some of the world's most famous beaches such as Copacabana and Ipanema. Other famous landmarks are the Sugar Loaf Mountain and the statue of Christ the Redeemer.

Rio de Janeiro

Santiago, Chile

Santiago, Chile

Santiago, the capital of Chile, is the 5th largest city in South America. Today, it is one of the most modern cities on the continent. Santiago is a cosmopolitan city and is the financial, cultural and political centre of the country.

Sao Paulo, Brazil

The capital of the State of São Paulo is the city of **São Paulo**. In Brazil, only the states of São Paulo and Rio de Janeiro

Sao Paulo, Brazil

have a capital city with the same name as the state.

The city is South America's largest, centre for trade and industry. Sao Paulo surprises all with its sheer size. With over 10 million inhabitants, it is the world's third largest city and the largest in South America. Sao Paulo and its rival Brazilian city, Rio de Janeiro, have often been compared to New York and Los Angeles respectively. If Rio has gained fame for its striking natural setting, Sao Paulo's attraction lies in its people and its vibrant cultures.

Bogota, Colombia

Bogota, Colombia

Nestled high in the Andes at 2620 m, **Santafé de Bogotá** is a city of contrasts. It's a city of high-rise buildings standing next to colonial churches and a city of universities and theatres. It is a mixture of Spanish and English and Indian. influences.

Lima, Peru

Lima, Peru

Lima is Peru's cultural and commercial centre. Lima runs at a slower pace than many South American metropolises; its rhythm is more traditional and its people reflect a steadier, calmer constitution. Lima's unusually amenable inhabitants give the metropolis the feeling, at times, of a cluster of smaller towns.

Several museums display and preserve Peru's golden past, including most notably the internationally famed Museo Nacional de Antropologiay Arqueologia.

Caracas, Venezuela

Venezuela's capital city sits about 914.4 m above sea level in a long valley. In recent decades, especially during oil booms of the 1970s and 80s, **Caracas** has seen unprecedented growth. Many of the original colonial buildings were replaced by gleaming modern skyscrapers. A majority of the cultural and architectural attractions can be found in the area immediately surrounding Plaza Bolivar, the city centre.

Cartagena, Colombia

Caracas, Venezuela

Cartagena, Colombia

It is also Columbia's premier tourist attraction. The city is connected by a series of bridges and divided by 17th century walls into an 'historic old city' and a cosmopolitan 'modern city'.

Hot, sultry, filled with the sounds of music and bright with colour and tradition, **Cartagena** has been an important port on the Caribbean since it was founded in 1533. Cartagena's colonial charm with tiled roofs, balconies and flower-filled courtyards, beckons visitors to walk the narrow streets or to enjoy a weekend getaway.

Quito, Ecuador

Ecuador's capital is a mix of colonial history and modern enterprise— a city in the middle of the world and a delight to visitors. **Quito** is the second highest capital in the world in respect to its geographical area. It is also one of South America's most entrancing cities, possessing a balmy climate, a wealth of fine Spanish colonial architecture, and a magnificent setting at the base of Pichincha volcano.

Quito is surrounded by natural beauty of mountains, lushly forested hills and a fertile valley. It was a major Inca city destroyed by the Incas and rebuilt by the Spanish invaders. Most visitors concentrate their time in Old Town, for which UNESCO named Quito a cultural heritage site in 1978.

Quito, Ecuador

Salvador, El Salvador

San Salvador, El Salvador

San Salvador is the capital and the largest city of the country. It is the centre of trade and communications.

San Salvador is the second biggest city in Central America. Island in the Bahamas, in the Caribbean Sea, is said to have been the island where the explorer Christopher Columbus first landed in the New World in 1492.

Salvador, El Salvador

ATLANTIC OCEAN
Gulf of Mexico
MEXICO
Hermosillo
Chihuahua
Guadalajara
Mexico City
Oaxaca
Merida
BAHAMAS
Nassau
Habana
CUBA
WEST INDIES
HAITI
Port-au-Prince
DOMINICAN REPUBLIC
Santo Domingo
San Juan
Puerto Rico
JAMAICA
Kingston
Belmopan
BELIZE
HONDURAS
Tegucigalpa
CENTRAL AMERICA
GUATEMALA
Guatemala
San Salvador
EL SALVADOR
NICARAGUA
Managua
COSTA RICA
San Jose
PANAMA
Panama City
Clipperton (Fr.)
CARIBBEAN SEA
BARBADOS
Bridgetown
Port of Spain
TRINIDAD & TOBAGO
Barranquilla
Maracaibo
Caracas
VENEZUELA
Cacuri
San Carlos
Georgetown
GUYANA
Lethem
Paramaribo
SURINAM
Cayenne
FRENCH GUIANA
Medellin
Bogota
COLOMBIA
Cali
Icana
Equator
Quito
ECUADOR
Guayaquil
Santa Maria
Belem
Amazon
Manaus
Fortaleza
PERU
Trujillo
Lima
Cruzeiro
BRAZIL
Abune
Recife
Salvador
Brasilia
Puno
La Paz
BOLIVIA
Sucre
Arica
Corumba
Filadelfia
PARAGUAY
Asuncion
Antofagasta
Rio de Janeiro
Sao Paulo
Curitiba
PACIFIC OCEAN
CHILE
ARGENTINA
Cordoba
Mendoza
Rosario
Porto Alegre
Salto
URUGUAY
Montevideo
Buenos Aires
Santiago
ATLANTIC OCEAN
Mar del Plata
Valdivia
Puerto Montt
Rawson
Santa Cruz
Falkland Islands (U.K.)
Tierra del Fuego
South Georgia (U.K.)

Test Your MEMORY

1. Which piece of land connects South America to North America?
2. Which country in South America falls under the control of the French government?
3. Name the world's longest mountain chain?
4. Which is the highest point in South America?
5. In which country of South America are the Angels Falls located?
6. Name the two weather phenomenon affecting the climate of South America.
7. In which year did Christopher Columbus reach South America?
8. When was total independence achieved by the South American countries?
9. Which countries are included in Latin America?
10. Who was named the 'football player of the century'?
11. What is the capital city of Argentina?
12. Which city has been nicknamed as the 'marvellous city'?

Index

* Maps not to scale; for illustration purpose only.